THE SOONER THE

An Anthology of Thank-Y(
edited by
Hugo Whately

The Phortse Project and The Gordon Daniel Memorial

Gordon Daniel was killed in a tragic accident at Eton College in November 1993. His family, friends and the school helped raise funds to build a memorial in his name. As Gordon would have been a member of the following year's *Towards Everest Expedition* in Nepal, it was decided to help a village community there. The members of that expedition played their part in building a medical centre which was opened in August 1994. It was decided that the remaining funds would be used in the second phase of the memorial; the building of a Gompa (or monastery-cum-community centre) in the same village. The village of Phortse comprises about forty Sherpa families, and is situated about twelve miles south of Mount Everest at 12,000ft up the Khumbu valley.

This summer a second Eton expedition is going to Phortse to finish the memorial. Money raised through the sale of this book will go firstly towards expedition costs, and once these are met, to the building of the Gompa. If you would like to order more copies of this book [price £3 inc p&p], or to contribute to the Gordon Daniel Memorial Fund please write to The Manor House, Holybourne, Alton, Hampshire GU34 4HD.

I would like to thank all of you who sent me letters, gave contributions and offered me advice including:
Mr and Mrs E Allhusen, Mr and Mrs M Amory, Mrs T Barrow, Mr and Mrs T Branfoot, Mrs P Breese, Mr and Mrs D Brooksbank, Mr and Mrs P Carmichael, Mr and Mrs T Drabble, Mr and Mrs J Evans, Mr and Mrs R Finlayson, Mrs M Fletcher, Mr and Mrs T Floyd, Mr and Mrs A Gardner, Miss R Goad, Mr and Mrs A Gordon Walker, Mr and Mrs R Graef, Mr and Mrs H Gunn, Mr and Mrs T Gutch, Mr and Mrs K Hall, Mr and Mrs G St J Hallett, Mr and Mrs G Higson, Mr and Mrs M Hutchings, Mr and Mrs T Instone, Mrs R Jenner-Fust, Mr and Mrs C Kilpatrick, Mr A Lyndon Skeggs, Mr and Mrs C Malden, Mr and Mrs I McNeil, Mr and Mrs A Neilson, Mr and Mrs R Neilson, Miss E Oxley, Mr and Mrs M Palau, Mr and Mrs C Pinney, Brigadier and Mrs P Prescott, Mrs A A Robertson, Mr and Mrs A Robertson, Mr and Mrs J Salkeld, Mr and Mrs L Seligman, Mr and Mrs M Sutherland, Mr and Mrs S Urry, Mr and Mrs D Whately, Miss A Whately, Mr and Mrs M White, Mr and Mrs A Wilson, Mrs S Whigham, The Rev Ben and Mrs Whitworth, and Mrs E Hutchison who gave me the motto:

> 'The sooner you write
> a bread and butter letter
> the better'

and hence the title of the book. I would also like to thank Nick Devereux for having. taken such trouble over the illustrations.

The Times Newspaper kindly sent me details of correspondence on the subject of thank you letters, and I would like to thank all those who wrote to The Times for allowing me to reproduce their letters here.

Due to the great response I'm afraid it was impossible to include all the contributions, but they were all much appreciated.

The Weald Printers got me off to a brilliant start by offering to print this book for a nominal sum and gave much advice along the way. I am particularly grateful to them.

I would also like to thank Mrs Beckwith-Smith's Charitable Settlement, The Southdown Trust, The Old Etonian Trust and the Herbert and Peter Blagrave Charitable Trust for their generous support.

Published by Weald Printers Ltd
Unit 3, Daux Road, Billingshurst
West Sussex RH14 9SJ

CONTENTS

INTRODUCTION

Some say that thank you letters are the bane of childhood, the sting in the tail that sours every happy occasion. But they are more than just this; they stay with us even in old age, they are the bane of our entire lives.

This, of course, isn't entirely true. Most people enjoy showing their appreciation and find that a letter is the best way to do it. Far better than using the telephone as you don't have to explain yourself or make polite conversation. It is also more gratifying to receive a letter as you can read it over and over again.

Having looked through hundreds of thank-you letters, I can now fully appreciate how much pleasure a good one gives. You can always tell when effort has been put into a letter and how sincere it is. The endless strings of adjectives that most of us tend to reel off are all very well, but there is no doubt in my mind that the best letters don't resort to this. Of the letters I have included, some are excellent, some are not quite so good and some are just rude. To the best of my knowledge they are all genuine, and the names, of course, have been changed to protect the innocent.

I have enjoyed putting this book together and the letters have given me many ideas. I hope you will enjoy reading it.

1

CHAPTER ONE

Letters to The Times

It was something of a co-incidence that the following correspondence was started in The Times by Mrs Corkery at the same time as I was preparing this book. The general feeling seems to be that thank-you letters are a thing of the past, and that fewer people are making the effort nowadays, however my experience is that the tradition is alive and well. The following letters certainly suggest that it is a topic which arouses much interest.

16th February 1996
Sir,
A letter arrived this morning from a five-year-old, thanking me for a lovely Christmas present and wishing me a Happy New Year. Remembering that a round of thank-you letters is a hard task for the young I was much impressed.
Later I realised that it was a photocopy with my name added in pencil.
Yours faithfully
Helen Corkery

20th February 1996
Sir,
My grandson, aged six, sent all his Christmas thank-you letters typed and printed on the family computer. He added his own pictures of Father Christmas and snowmen. I feel that this is a very acceptable way of keeping an old tradition alive in a modern context and I was very pleased to receive my copy.
Yours faithfully
Jean Stephenson

20th February 1996
Sir,
Mrs Helen Corkery's letter about the ingenious five-year-old and his photocopied thank-you letter reminded me of the last day of term, 30 years ago, when I nervously handed in 1,000 lines well earned no doubt. The task consisted of one page of 50 lines, photocopied on the relatively new device 20 times. It was accepted without demur; but my fellow miscreant, more diligent than I and without access to the labour-saving device, sought redress in the playground shortly after.
Yours faithfully,
David Smith

23rd February 1996
Sir,
Perhaps the solution to extracting thank-you letters from children is to make it clear that no letter of thanks means no present next time. This should also apply to adults receiving presents from children.
Yours faithfully
Rebekah Budenberg

23rd February 1996
Sir,
With a little more hardware added to his computer, Mrs Jean Stephenson's grandson could have sent his thank-you letters by e-mail or fax, so avoiding the equally old tradition of an invigorating walk to the post-box.
Yours faithfully
David J Powell

23rd February 1996
Sir,
In our heritage-conscious times is saying thank-you now to be regarded [Mrs Stephenson's letter] as "an old tradition"?
Yours faithfully,
Jennifer Donkin

14th February 1996
Sir,
The solution to extracting thank-you letters is that which is followed by my octogenarian grandmother.
Not having received a thank-you letter from her graceless grandson for 25 years she sent my last Christmas present with a pre-written thank-you letter and a stamped addressed envelope.
I think I was meant to sign and return it.
Yours faithfully
Caspar Glyn

28th February 1996
Sir,
Perhaps those letter writers criticising computer thank-you letters should show a bit of old-fashioned courtesy themselves by receiving them with pleasure instead of criticism. They might receive more!
Manners are taught as much by example as by the telling.
Yours faithfully,
Adrienne Capron-Tee

2nd March 1996

Sir,

To extract a letter of thanks one could follow the example of Andrew Carnegie, as recounted in Joseph Frazier Wall's 1970 biography.

When his sister-in-law complained to him that her son, his namesake, never wrote to her while he was away at college, Mr Carnegie confidently bet her ten dollars that he could get an answer by return mail.

The wager was accepted, and Mr Carnegie sat down and wrote a newsy letter to young Andrew, ending with a postscript that he was enclosing a $10 bill as a little gift. But he deliberately omitted to enclose the money.

Within two days there was a letter of thanks pointing out Mr Carnegie's "mistake". This was of course rectified with the winnings from the bet.

Yours sincerely,

Fred Mann

6th March 1966

Sir,

My most successful thank-you letter was also the least arduous.

I had received a book for Christmas which contained the Nigel Molesworth Self-Adjusting Thank You Letter. It began, if my memory serves:

Dear aunt/uncle/penpal/stinker/clot,

Thank you for your present. I have played with constantly/broken it already/got three more like it.

I typed up numerous carbon copies with suitable adapted working, crossed out bits and sent them off. To my amazement, I received several replies, the only time I got thank-you letters for a thank-you letter.

Yours faithfully,

P R Shortell

6th March 1966

Sir,

There is a cheaper alternative to Andrew Carnegie's method of extracting a letter from a reluctant correspondent.

During the last war the mother of a friend of mine was in despair at never hearing from him. She wrote to him saying that if she didn't have a reply within the next week she would ask Sandy Powell on the forces programme to play a tune for him with the message, "Please write home to your mother".

Many years later I employed the same device with one of my sons away at school only substituting the Jimmy Young show. Reply came by return post.

Yours faithfully,

Angela Willbourn.

CHAPTER TWO

Thank-you letters for presents

Thank you letters for Birthday or Christmas presents are always much easier to write if they are something you've always wanted, or something you can put straight into your bank account. But the trouble starts when you really have to think about your letter and say something sensible. These letters that follow have done just this.

The opening lines are often considered to be the most important. This one has an instantly light hearted, but none the less appreciative feel to it.

Dear Harriet
CASH!!! HOORAY!!! I mean thank you for the lettuce. . . .

This writer, although slightly over the top, is certain to receive another present next year.

To my dear and most generous Uncle Henry,
Until I received your letter by this morning's post I did not for one moment believe it was possible for joy and happiness of such immeasurable magnitude to be contained within a simple envelope. . . .

We can either interpret this next letter as a genuine loss for words, or indeed pure laziness.

Dear Godfather John,
WOW!
Love Edward

The sixteen year old who wrote this has done particularly
well by sharing the fun of the spending.

Dear Ruth

Thank you so much for the cheque. I could've used it to save my ailing financial
predicament, but as it was, fickle thing that I am, I've spent it already.
I went down to the King's Road with a couple of friends intending just to watch them
shop and enjoy themselves but I ended up buying a pair of jeans (second-hand,
green, faded, as you can probably imagine I look unbelievably good in them) costing
somewhat conveniently £20, so thank you. . . .

This excellent letter is from a 13 year old:

Dear Godpa Rufus

Thank you very much for the torch and the cufflinks. The torch is really useful
especially with the bendy extension. It's really good for reading with it on. I tested
it on Friday night. However I think I read a bit too much as I was really tired on
Saturday.
The cufflinks are really nice and Daddy says I shouldn't wear them until I am older.
According to my brother if I took them to school I would lose them straight away.
But I'm really looking forward to wearing them for the first time.
Thanks for being such a great godparent for the past 13 years. Thanks again for the
great presents.
Love from Jamie

This letter from a fourteen year old solves problems that would leave most of us at a loss for words.

Darling Godmama Caroline,
Thank you very much for the absolutely wonderful thing. Did it come from Pakistan by any chance? What on earth was it FOR? I have broken it already, of course, but I love you for sending it and it was marvellous while it lasted. Perhaps such a beautiful loony object is not designed to be long for this wicked earth and is just supposed to be fun until it dies? Just like me. Anyway, I buried it today, because it was so far from home. So there's some part of Cornwall that is forever Karachi or wherever you went.
Do you still promise to take me one day?
We had a great Christmas and sorry this letter is so late, nearly the end of February already. Must run,
lots of love Jemma xxxxxx ooooooo

But it's young childrens letters that are often the most pleasing. This writer is eight:

Dear Jane
Thank you very much for my Fimo. I think it is simply great stuff. So far I have made a mug, a tiny broach, and a marble ball. I think the next thing I make will be for you. Please write a note saying what you want. Hope you had a lovely Christmas. Lots of love Charlie.

and this one is eleven:

Dear Victoria
Than you very much for our Easter egg. It is not quite the sort we like! But I dare say the inhabitants of this wicked house will gobble it up quickly! It was very kind of you to bother. Please come and eat some more ice cream soon.
Lots of love Leonie

This boy is six:

Darling Godmother Sara
Thank you for the ruksak and canteen. I have been hiking through the house for days.

And here is an appreciative letter from a young writer thanking for a Jenners Token:

Thank you for being my god mother. I'll never forget the first time we met when mum went base over apex in the rowing boat on your loch— not sunny really but what a laugh. Your Jenners Token is burning a hole in my pocket. Mum is taking me into town next saturday. I'll let you know what I by. A big thank you.

Unfortunately it's also the young childrens letters that tend to be the most direct. I'm sure that there are quite a number of caring godparents out there who have been put down in the same way as these have:

Dear Aunt Daisy
Thank you so much for the book about gym. I've put it on the shelf with all my other books about gym. . . .

Dear Uncle Tom
     Thank you for the
~~£10~~ £5 you gave me for
my birthday

Dear Godfather Richard,

Thank you for the lovely riding gloves. They are very nice and will do very well as a spare pair as my godmother gave me nicer ones, which I will use for best.

CHAPTER THREE

Thank-you letters for holidays and visits

This was one of the best opening lines I found, simple yet effective:

Dear Powells

Thank you so much for having me to stay in August, It was easily the best week of the holidays. We managed to cram so much into such a short time. . . .

There is a fine line between going over the top and not going far enough with your thanks. This letter has the perfect balance, they don't get much better than this for appreciation.

Dear Mr. and Mrs. Bridges

I think it would be hard for the greatest writers to express the enjoyment I had with you in Chalet Fleuris and on the slopes of Klosters last week. It was an incredible holiday and I regularly find myself wishing I could reverse time back to 04:30 on the 27th December before I set off. I think my final day, as I strapped my feet into my bindings and began to sift down the deserted slopes from the top station, will never be forgotten in all my snowboarding days. The cool, silent feel of the powder spraying up in my face as I veered off the piste, the only sound being of the soft thump behind me as it fell down again after each wide turn. Snowboarding has been my favourite thing in the world and you generously provided me with a fantastic holiday.

Thank you all very much indeed. With love Ralph

This line was just slipped in at the end of a letter:

Thank you so much, I'm coming again whether you ask me or not.

Children often manage to add a very personal touch to their letters and here are two perfect examples:

Thank you so much for letting me come and stay I really enjoyed it I loved sleeping in a four poster bed and thank you for the famous five game I have not yet found the treasure but I hope I do I love your cooking I wish my mum could cook like you) I really liked making those apple pies.

Dear Granny and Grandpa

Thank you very much for the fabulos holiday at knoll. I always look foreward to it and it is never a disipountment. I love seeing you, especially, and every one else.

I really enjoy the golf. It is always so much more fun with you than with any other people eg: peter. I don't know why but it just is.

Tomorow I'm going to football prachise and after that I'm going to go gocarting It is very sad that the holidays are ending.

Of course, the longer you leave it the harder a letter is to write. This late letter must have been good to receive:

My humblest apologies for yet another late letter of thanks. My weekend at your home was one of sedate pleasure, my favourite kind now I settle into a calm middle-age at nineteen. The weather, company and setting wanted for nothing, indeed I believe you set a new standard for entertaining at home.

I know I shall be seeing you again soon, and look forward to it.

19

Thank you poems will always be appreciated if only because of the effort that must have gone into them.

Seven Days Skiing

I came by plane, they said "No snow"
"Just wind and rain" But don't you know
I skiied the piste in mountains fair
For on the hills That had been bare
The snow came down To oblige me
Though not in town - that's Champéry -
I drank up sun, I skiied, and fell
I had great fun And I'm still well.
We played 'up yours' - The game I mean-
And amid snores discussed benzene
Once more thank you For a cool week
A good chance to improve technique
I must end here, Oh! One more thing
Later this year come windsurfing

It has to be said that this letter was one of the best I came across. It's a clever and witty way of expressing thanks.

Dear Alec and Louise

It may interest you to know that my recent stay in your delightful home was rather more than a purely social exercise. I am actually working on behalf of the " European Guests' Charter Commission ". The commission has been created by the government in order to regulate " Hosts ", as previously anybody could set themselves up as a " Host " regardless of qualifications.

You were judged on a number of criteria, which I have laid out below along with your corresponding grade and comments.

1. Warmth of greeting

B+

Would have been an A had Alec recognised me at the airport.

2. " At ease " rating

A+

Very high rating due to your suppressing laughter/annoyance at my

a) Failure to distinguish between milk and buttermilk and adding the latter to my tea

b) Losing a vital piece of paper with directions on that had been painstakingly researched by Louise and then complaining when I caught the wrong tram in the wrong direction to the wrong place

c) Failure to wake up until Sunday lunch time and therefore sleeping through church

3. Food and Drink

A++

Seat moved to rear of plane on return journey as ballast due to irresistibility of risotto. Also unique experience of eyeballs attempting to change sockets as a direct result of the potency of the Williams' gin and tonic

4. Tact

E-

Low mark due to embarrassment at airport caused by my tears and Alec's insistence that I wave all the way down the escalator.

****

You will be pleased to hear that you are therefore recognised as Grade I with distinction hosts and will shortly be receiving your certificate of authentication. Your name has been entered into the " Let's Go Europe " guide and you should be receiving your first dozen Norwegian students any minute now!

Much love Emily

CHAPTER FOUR

Thank-you letters for parties

```
Writing about a party is possibly the most difficult
thing to do well.  Indeed this is where most of us settle
for the second class letter, and the endless strings of
well meant adjectives start to flow. The result is often
good enough, but these that follow seem to go a stage
further:
```

Dear Mrs and all the Martins,
WOW
The postman must be dragging mail sacks to your door. You must be reading heaps
of letters all of which visibly indicate the authors' grappling with his/her old/young
imagination searching to produce an original, memorable way of saying "I had a
lovely time", a sentiment felt by hundreds of minds which still haven't fully
recovered from the Party. Perhaps some of your enchanted guests still haven't quite
got down to earth. . . .

Dear Susie and Jeremy,
What a fantastic and amazing party - it really was THE PARTY OF 1995. I cannot
think how you ever managed to sort out all those people, get them fed, seated, into
house parties - decorate the marquee so beautifully and still be the perfect hostess -
appearing to have not a care in the world. Well done - the best feat of organisation
I've ever seen. Felix and I felt extremely honoured to be part of such a happy
occasion, and thank you and Jeremy for including us in your festivities. We couldn't
have enjoyed it more - although Felix did complain bitterly about having to put on
black tights!
Our house-party were charming - particularly Richard Bramer, who won millions of
Brownie Points when we found him washing-up the breakfast, after the girls - he can
come again any time!
Again lots of thanks for such a fun evening. Lots of love
Jessica

Dearest Susie,
For the better part of this glorious summer, Wiltshire has been talking about the Martin's party. It was a truly magnificent feat to carry it off so brilliantly after such a crescendo of anticipation. There will be as many after waves of happy memories as there were before's slightly worried "What shall I wear's"
The noise of sheer happiness was so wonderful and I know that went on until very very late hours. Thank you all for a wonderful evening so beautifully organized.
With love from us both
Rosalie.

Dear Mr and Mrs Martin
Thank you, albeit very belatedly, for your lovely party back in September. Coming, as it did, right at the end of the summer, it was a very nice opportunity to meet up friends after travels, meet new friends for the coming year off and have a last tango before the rigours of the rat race. After the excesses of the post-A-level summer, anything less than an awesome party would have been an anti-climax. Yours did not disappoint. Never have I been to a party where much an effort has been made but not only by the hosts, but also all the guests. It meant that everyone - from the first moment they put on their wonderful costumes, or first saw the lasers from the motorway - was up for a good time. My enduring memory of it shall be the huge dining room with circular tables crammed with faces one hadn't seen for years, with old and new friends. It was one of those parties one comes away from feeling very popular because so many agreeable people one knew were there, and everyone was in such good form.
Thank you so much for setting a precedent.
Yours sincerely
Adrian

Dear Mr and Mrs Martin

I am just writing to thank you very much indeed for the amazing party last Saturday. I had never been to anything like it before in my life, in terms of both scale and style!

Everything and everyone looked incredible, and I had a great time. Eating breakfast in the garden at some ridiculous hour of the early morning is one moment that will really stay with me.

Thank you very much again for such a good night.

Love Venetia

Two different views of the same party show that the truth isn't always the best thing to say. These were from 12 year olds:

Dear Mrs Allen

I'm sorry it's taken me such a long time to write, but thank you so much for having me to Orlando's party - it was really great fun. I thought the DJ was especially good - he played all the best stuff for dancing to. It was great to see everyone before going back to school and to find out what they'd been doing etc.

Thank you so much

Lots of love Nicholas

Dear Orlando

Thank you very much for the party. I enjoyed it a lot. Pity the DJ ran out of music and ended up playing a few pieces again and again.

I thought it was a success.

From Daniel

Thank you so much for inviting me to such a brilliant party. It was very funny seeing everyone looking so different dressed in 50's/60's costume! although several people gave me some rather strange looks on the train down to you!! I always feel that partys are going to be absolutely terrifying and that I will just end up giggling rather shyly in the corner with someone I don't really want to be with, but your annual party completely destroys that image and is great fun!

Excuses for late letters are often painfully transparent. This one deals with the problem rather well particularly as the writer had met his hosts several times since the party.

Dear Mr and Mrs James,

I am extremely embarrassed about the lateness of this letter. I have, for the past month, been on an exchange to Burma to sharpen up my knowledge of a local dialect. My Bundachingfilopinise has now reached a satisfactory level of competence. Due to the lack of postal services I'm afraid I could only write once I got back to England. I hear my exchange, Rajit, looks rather like me and I hope he has had a satisfactory stay.

The party was one to remember and I think the one I have most enjoyed. It was very stylish and has set the tone for numerous 18ths to come. I doubt they will better that wonderful night. Thank you so much for a great time and I'm sorry about the absurd lateness of the letter.

Yours Rudolf

Good opening paragraphs thanking for an eighteenth party:

Dear Mrs Everett,

I don't think I've been to such a spectacular party ever. Thank you so much for giving us all a fabulous time. . . .

Thank you very much for organising and hosting the party last night. It was, without a doubt, one of the best parties I have ever been to and needless to say I thoroughly enjoyed myself. The food was delicious and my glass was seldom empty!

Well what can I say? If ever there was a greater party I'd be surprised.

Thank you for organising such an epic party to celebrate Sam's eighteenth. It was incredible to find that from the moment I accepted your kind invitation everything had been taken care of from the times of the trains and transport from the station, to my other dinner guests and extremely comfortable accommodation. I was able to enjoy myself fully without needing to worry about a thing.

How can a letter describe the enjoyment of a party? In this case it can't but I shall try.

Thanks for such an excellent party. Never has my internal timeclock suffered so much - breakfast at 3 am - I'm used to having it nearer to 3 pm! Champagne before breakfast - dancing during breakfast - even conversation at breakfast!

Thank you very much for inviting me to Sam's party. It was a brilliant success, so much so that it is still being talked about and the gossip has still not died down.

Although I'm sure these two letters meant well, they are
unfortunately slightly rude. Definitely examples of
things not to say.

Dear Mr and Mrs Rotherwick
Thanks so much for such a wonderful party, which was even bigger and better than
last year.
I really enjoyed the BBQ even though I missed it and ate dinner at 2am.
Thanks once again
Love Julian

Dear Mr and Mrs Rotherwick,
Thank you so much for such a wonderful party. This one was much better than last
year's.
I hope you won the cricket on Sunday. I'm sure I'll see Harry again soon.
Thanks again. Walter

This letter is thanking for a wedding at which Donald,
who wrote the letter, made a speech:

My dear Andrew
That was really a tremendously successful event and before even thanking you for
the mink-lined basket you contrived to find for M and myself, many congratulations
to you both on such superb stage-management of [always] a difficult event. Our
time will come, no doubt - and tho' they talk of "doing it quietly" and "just a few
friends", well enough do I realise it will have to be like that, and we shall clearly
have to take your production as a model. It seemed to me so admirable to avoid that
managerial manner of the Chadwick Marquee Company Inc coupled with Delicacies
International, and to have an efficient, family-run show.
All that apart, we thought well of the place you got us our head down, and I have just
written a breathy, slightly illiterate and ecstatic b & b to our hostess which I hope
will give pleasure.
Love and thanks to your both,
Yours ever, Donald.

Dear Melanie,

What a magical day today! Thank you so much for the delicious lunch - so relaxed and it was like another world - almost continental outside at that big table in such glorious surroundings- and all your wonderful hospitality. The shooting was enormous fun and the whole afternoon will be remembered with great pleasure for a long time.

Very many thanks,

Yours, Rebecca.

CHAPTER FIVE

Miscellaneous thank-you letters

This is a rare example of a letter thanking for a letter, although unfortunately it's not a particularly cheerful one:

Darling Lara

What a superb letter - Grandpa and I were delighted to hear from you, but very sad to hear about your ankle. Its jolly painful I know. When I was about 11 years old I did the same and you will never guess why! My sister dared me to try and get round our bedroom without touching the floor - I was doing fine until I stood on a small shelf which gave way and I fell. Very stupid, but I didn't think!! Lesley is going into hospital in about a weeks time - she has been in a lot of pain, so I am sure a letter from you will really cheer her up.

Grandpa and I are not too bad, but I may have to have another operation on my leg as one of the screws in my leg has slipped! Anyway keep your fingers crossed and send good luck thoughts and I may be OK.

Get well soon Lara and enjoy the rest of the term. Easter Hols will soon be here, and you want to be quite fit again.

Lots of love

Granny

I liked this one:

Darling,

How generous of you to send so many red roses to the office with a note saying that I was wonderful. Thank goodness we both know that now, as do the five hundred people in my business life, who have mentioned it in passing daily, for the last week. To have been a pin-striped, ten-day wonder has been a nightmare. Thank God I am on my way back to Oman at last. I will thank you never to thank me again but I thank you for thanking me unforgettably. I feel thanked up to here.

Very much love Hugh

Although I doubt the authenticity of this letter, I expect it rings bells for many of us.

My Dear Zoe

Thank you for your letter, which arrived this morning. It was lovely to see you again at Christmas and I hope the holiday made the long journey home and back worth while. We did at least know that you had enough petrol for the return trip as the account from the garage arrived yesterday; it's amazing the amount that little car of yours holds.

Whilst I think of it, could you see if you packed my hair dryer by mistake? I have looked in your room and, apart from my nail scissors, razor and green shirt which were under the bed, the only other thing which appears to be missing is my dressing gown. Oh, and don't worry about the carpet. As you say, it was coffee coloured to start with and I can always move the dressing table over the stain if it doesn't fade.

No, we haven't got a lot of the Christmas goodies left - in fact apart from a few hard centre chocolates with teeth marks in them and some plain liquorice all sorts, everything seems to have gone. Were the sherry truffles as good as they looked?

I took your book back to the library and tried to explain that you didn't drop it in the bath deliberately but you know how haughty the assistant with the frizzy hair can be. I suppose they will put the money towards a replacement. I know what you mean about baths being so relaxing and there's no need to feel guilty.

Thanks for making a start on taking down the decorations. I have finally finished the job and agree with you that in future sticky tape is best avoided. I did find, however, that not quite so much wallpaper came away, if the tape was removed slowly.

Give my love to Mel. It was nice to meet her, and of course I don't blame her for the cigarette burn on the bedside table. It could have happened to anyone.

Now darling, you mentioned something about a weekend in March. Your father and I would love to see you, of course, but it looks as though we may be away for a short break ourselves. I would suggest leaving the key and you could come anyway, but I know how you hate cooking and washing. Perhaps we could arrange something in the summer?

Fondest love Mummy

However the final contribution I have received supports some of the views expressed in The Times, and suggests that perhaps thank-you letters are becoming a thing of the past in today's busy life.

Darling, please don't write. I won't have time to read it.